Still as a Mountain,
Powerful as Thunder

Calligraphy: *the fire of life*

Still as a Mountain, Powerful as Thunder

Simple Taoist Exercises for Healing,
Vitality, and Peace of Mind

Y. P. DONG

SHAMBHALA

Boston & London

1993

Shambhala Publications, Inc.
Horticultural Hall
300 Massachusetts Avenue
Boston, Massachusetts 02115

© 1993 by Y. P. Dong

Calligraphies by Y. P. Dong

Photographs by Mark Greenberg

9   8   7   6   5   4   3

Printed in the United States of America
⊗ This edition is printed on acid-free paper that meets the
American National Standards Institute Z39.48 Standard.

Distributed in the United States by Random House, Inc., and in
Canada by Random House of Canada Ltd

Library of Congress Cataloging-in-Publication Data

Dong, Y. P.
    Still as a mountain, powerful as thunder: simple Taoist exercises
for healing, vitality, and peace of mind / Y.P. Dong. — 1st ed.
        p.   cm.
    ISBN 0-87773-688-X (alk. paper)
    1. Exercise.   2. Taoism.   I. Title.   II. Title: Simple Taoist
exercises for healing, vitality, and peace of mind.
GV481.D66   1993   92-50442
613.7'148—dc20   CIP

Contents

7   *Acknowledgments*

11   *Introduction*

15   PART ONE   *The Art of I Chuan*

17   The Benefits of I Chuan

19   An Ancient Solution to a Modern Problem

26   Master Wang and the Origin of I Chuan

29   Principles of I Chuan Practice

30   Where, When, and How to Practice

32   Guidelines for Practice

34   Focusing the Mind

37   PART TWO   *Beginner's Exercises*

38   1. Flood Dragon Emerges from the Water

40   2. Heaven and Earth Sink and Float

42   3. Two Baby Swallows Flying

44   4. Pick a Star from the Pleiades

46   5. Stand on the Earth and Hold the Heavens

48   6. Pull the Ox Tail Back

50   7. Spring Silkworms Spin Silk

52   8. Push Two Horses Back

54   9. Two Hands Grasp Emptiness

56   10. Small T'ai Chi Circle

58   11. Circling Left and Right

60   12. Open and Close the Tan-t'ien

63   PART THREE   *Advanced Meditation Exercises*

65   I Chuan and Taoist Alchemy

70   Principles of Standing Meditation

72   Sitting Meditation

74   Standing Meditation 1

75   Standing Meditation 2

77   PART FOUR   *Drawing Power from Nature*

84   The Practice of the Sun

85   The Practice of the Moon

86   The Practice of the Mountain and Stones

88   The Practice of the Trees

90   The Practice of the Wind and Rain

91   The Practice of the Water

92   The Practice of the Rainbow

93   PART FIVE   *Exercises for Common Problem Areas*

94   Heart

97   Knees

100   Back

103   Stomach

105   Sexual Energy

108   Headache

109   Sinuses

111   *About the Author*

Acknowledgments

This book is dedicated to the memory of:
> Grand Master Wang Xiang Zhai
> Master Zhang Chang Xing
> Master Yu Peng Xi

I extend special thanks to Jonathan Blank and Barclay Powers, whose assistance was instrumental in the production of this book.

I also wish to thank Rebecca Painter and Alexander Lim for their help.

I am also grateful to my wife and my parents for all their support.

Still as a Mountain,
Powerful as Thunder

Introduction

My art breaks new pathways—
It empowers every tendon and fills each
    bone with wondrous spirit.
Still as the leopard perched high before his
    attack,
It springs in coiling waves like a dragon.
Its ch'i makes a long rainbow that touches
    the sun,
Wanting to swallow the whole world into its
    stomach.
Commanding the wind and clouds, making
    dragons and serpents pale with fear,
The power of this art reverberates beyond
    the heavens.
Felt from afar as men hear lightning and
    thunder,
It exhales and inhales an ethereal air that
    envelops the universe—
In the great kiln of its fire all creatures are
    remolded,
Heaven and earth re-created.
                   —Wang Xiang Zhai

The place: Peking. The year: 1959. The event: a rare Chinese national martial arts competition. Government officials, teaching masters, and students of the martial arts at all levels of skill gather to watch the greatest fighters of their time compete. After many arduous matches, a champion emerges. But his satisfaction at this triumphant moment is not complete. He must find a man who is said to be the greatest living master—a man the national champion must defeat before he can believe in his official first place status.

At first glance, there is nothing unusual about this story. That is, until you learn that the man the young challenger sought out was Wang Xiang Zhai, the seventy-three-year-old founder of the I Chuan method of physical and mental development. Though in the West it seems strange for a young athlete to challenge an old man to a test of strength and agility, in the Chinese martial arts tradition, advanced age does not imply declining power. On the contrary, if their mastery is genuine, great masters become more powerful with age.

The reasons for this lie in the secrets of Chinese internal, or "soft," martial art forms that develop a type of strength that does not fade with age but rather grows even stronger. Even at the advanced age of seventy-three, Master Wang's highly developed internal force rendered the younger athlete's strength and skill completely useless.

During his life, Master Wang simplified and modified traditional martial art forms and created the internal form called I Chuan ("Mind Pugilism") as the logical culmination of exercises dating back to the Sung dynasty (960–1280 C.E.). The above incident illustrates the efficacy and power of his art. But don't be misled by the term *martial art*. The primary goal of I Chuan is to improve one's overall mental and physical health, vitality, stamina, resistance to disease, peace of mind, and energy for the tasks of daily life. The slow, rhythmic exercises combined with sitting and standing meditation postures outlined in this book provide a complete and highly effective means of developing internal energy, relaxing the mind, and strengthening the body. The effectiveness of the exercises stems from the combination of advanced Taoist breathing with focused, nonstressful isometrics.

I Chuan can be practiced by people of virtually any age, no matter what their life-style or state of health. Consistent practice of the exercises detailed in this book will yield noticeable results within a few weeks.

The reader should note that it is always best to practice I Chuan under the guidance of an expert instructor, who can ensure that the practitioner is progressing in a manner appropriate to his or her potential. However, the exercises in this book can be practiced safely by anyone provided that one does not overtrain and carefully follows the instructions and recommendations in this book.

The reader is advised to review this book several times in order to fully assimilate all the information it contains. Any questions may be directed to the author in care of the publisher:

> Master Y. P. Dong
> c/o Shambhala Publications, Inc.
> P.O. Box 308
> Boston, MA 02117

PART ONE
The Art of I Chuan

Calligraphy: ch'i

The Benefits of I Chuan

In the past ten years, many books and articles have been published about the "internal" martial arts. Internal martial arts, such as I Chuan or T'ai Chi Chuan, differ from external styles, such as Karate or Tae Kwon Do, in that muscular strength is not used. The training exercises emphasize breathing and smooth, relaxed movement as opposed to the straining muscular contraction necessary for the external forms. Many traditional martial arts include some internal power training, but it is usually reserved for a few of the most advanced students, who have proven themselves after ten or twenty years of devoted practice. Neither the published materials nor the closely guarded secrets of specialized arts provide a reliable way for the average layperson or martial arts student to acquire the benefits of authentic training in these disciplines.

I Chuan is a unique system of internal training that has recently become available in the West. It provides almost immediate results and can be practiced by people of all ages and levels of martial and athletic ability. By practicing I Chuan regularly for even less than a year, one can go from weakness to strength, from sickness to vibrant health. If one is already strong and healthy, one can become much stronger. Practicing this art can help people with such chronic conditions as high blood pressure, heart problems, asthma, weight problems, diabetes, sleeplessness, nervousness, bad memory, and bad appetite. It will also give one a healthier and more vibrant appearance.

Going to the doctor is passive treatment. To practice I Chuan is to take control of one's health. It can therefore be regarded as preventive medicine. For office workers, a half-hour in the morning or evening is all that is needed to increase energy and overcome stress. For older people the practice is good for the nervous system, metabolism, and circulation. In fact, everyone who practices these exercises will experience their benefits. The following are a few examples of I Chuan students who have been greatly helped by their practice.

Anthony, a forty-eight-year-old owner of a gas station, had suffered for many years with pain in his left knee. Finally, the chronic injury worsened, and as his pain increased, he was forced to walk with a pronounced limp. Six months after taking up I Chuan, his condition was dramatically improved. Anthony was able to walk normally and no longer felt any pain in his knee.

Susan, a sixty-eight-year-old retired professor, was beginning to feel the effects of old age. She often experienced dizzy spells and various digestive problems. Susan also had severe high blood pressure, a poor appetite, and a stiff gait requiring a cane. After six months of I Chuan practice, her blood pressure had returned to normal and she felt healthy and energetic. She also threw away her cane.

Gary was an executive at a major New York investment banking firm who had begun to experience a general lack of sexual vitality as well as premature ejaculation. He practiced the exercises outlined in this book for six months and his sexual functioning returned to normal.

The exercises described in this book will immediately have a noticeable effect on one's energy level, flexibility, and physical strength. The practitioner will become firmly balanced and rooted, as if deeply connected to the earth. While becoming physically stronger, the practitioner will also become more relaxed, with a smooth kind of power that is quite different from the tense, muscular strength developed by such external exercises as calisthenics, weightlifting, or Karate.

The advanced meditation and visualization techniques presented in this book provide the reader with an excellent method for developing mental control and inner stillness—essential elements of I Chuan. Without proper development of the mental aspect of training, the physical aspects lose much of their value. I Chuan is ultimately a highly developed exercise form that combines the mental and physical aspects of internal Chinese martial arts training, with each one effectively complementing and reinforcing the other.

AN ANCIENT SOLUTION TO A MODERN PROBLEM

When human beings are born, they are tender and soft. At death they are stiff and hard. All things, the grass as well as the trees, are tender and supple while alive. When dead they are withered and dried. Therefore, the stiff and hard are companions of death. The tender and soft are companions of life.

—Lao-tzu

The key to correct exercise begins with the connective tissue. Connective tissue includes the tendons, ligaments, and cartilage—the important elements of our joints. All physical movement is controlled by the way the body is connected at the joints, and so they are the key to balance, coordination, and physical strength. As children, we have an abundance of natural energy, which allows us both to grow and to remain flexible and supple. As the body ages, it stiffens and becomes more susceptible to injuries. The stiffness experienced by the elderly happens because the connective tissue in the joints has atrophied.

Unfortunately, problems with the joints may arise

even while we are in our prime. In 1986, the U.S. Bureau of Labor Statistics reported that the leading cause of occupational illness among both blue- and white-collar workers was repetitive strain injury— damage to the connective tissue, most notably in the hands, elbows, shoulders, neck, and back, caused by repetitive tasks.

I Chuan, with its smooth, flowing exercises and deep breathing, is an extremely effective means of vitalizing and strengthening connective tissue. Instead of merely toning the body's muscles, I Chuan develops connective tissue while stretching the muscular structure, greatly improving flexibility, balance, coordination, and athletic performance.

I Chuan is based upon the development of the body's inner energy, or ch'i. Traditional Chinese medicine views good health and long life as the result of a strong and balanced flow of energy within the body. Through I Chuan the body's natural energy level and immune functions are enhanced, often resulting in the complete cure of chronic spine and joint injuries, as well as a variety of illnesses in the respiratory, circulatory, gastrointestinal, and nervous systems.

As the American fitness trend continues to spread, more and more people have become interested in improving their health through regular exercise. Many of the physical problems that affect men and women as they age can be greatly reduced by a regular fitness program. But as people try to whip their bodies into shape with strenuous exercise and dieting, a number of new physical problems are emerging. The American Medical Association has discovered that stress is one of the most physically damaging consequences of modern life. Unfortunately, the majority of people who exercise are merely increasing the amount of stress that their bodies are already forced to endure on a daily basis. René Cailliet, M.D., an authority on sports medicine, states in his book *The Rejuvenation Strategy*: "Not a week goes by that I don't see a minimum of three new patients suffering from exercise-induced injuries. Significantly, nine out of ten of these patients are thirty-five or older. Exercise related injuries have reached epidemic proportions. I am not speaking of sports-related injuries. I am speaking of injuries incurred while trying to get into shape."

Running is considered by many people as the ideal way to get in shape, yet it exemplifies the potential dangers associated with exercise. Statistics show that over 50 percent of runners end up with knee and back problems. The U.S. Navy has advised officers over fifty to avoid jogging, because so many have suffered heart attacks as a result of this stressful form of exercise.

Weightlifters tear muscles, often damaging their joints and spine. Tennis, squash, and racquetball players injure their elbows and knees. Most alarmingly, many of those who begin exercising later in life develop permanent spinal problems and arthritic conditions as a direct result of improper exercise. A number of recent studies by sports medicine researchers have revealed that the benefits of aerobics are outweighed by the potential for injury. The general consensus among the American medical community is that a majority of back, hip, and knee problems in the United States results from injuries or muscular imbalances created through high intensity aerobic conditioning. The younger the body is, the more abuse it can take from hard exercises. Unfortunately, the damaging consequences of such exercises will probably not become evident until it is too late.

Yet exercise is essential to a healthy lifestyle. The *New England Journal of Medicine* published the results of a study on the connection between life expectancy and physical exercise among men. The study was based on information gathered from almost seventeen thousand alumni of Harvard University, whose ages at the start of the study ranged from thirty-five to seventy-four. The study concluded that alumni mortality rates were significantly lower among the physically active. The general findings were as follows:

- Men who exercised regularly reduced their risk of dying from major diseases.
- Men with hypertension who exercised regularly reduced their death rate by half.
- Regular exercise reduced mortality rates 25 percent among men either or both of whose parents died before the age of sixty-five and 50 percent among men whose parents lived beyond sixty-five.
- The more a man exercised, the better his longevity prospects. Among men who walked nine or more miles a week, the mortality rate was 21 percent lower than among men who walked three miles or less. Among men who engaged in light sports one or two hours a week, life expectancy was 24 percent greater than among those who did nothing.

Although this study did not measure the effects of exercise on women, it is no doubt safe to assume that the benefits of regular exercise for women would be comparable.

Western medicine has only recently begun to acknowledge that certain kinds of regular physical activity can slow down or even reverse the effects of aging. Long before Western medicine even existed, a science of physical exercise for health and longevity had been established in China. An ancient text, *The Spring and Autumn of the Lu Family* (249 B.C.E.), notes:

> Running water is never stale and a door hinge never gets worm-eaten, for they keep moving. The same applies to the human body. Without movement of the human body, the vital energy which maintains

the functioning of the body will not circulate, and without the circulation of this energy, life will stagnate and fail.

One has only to enter any park in Hong Kong, China, or Taiwan at five or six A.M. to see the difference between Chinese and American approaches to fitness. Scores of men and women, both young and old, gather every morning to invigorate themselves and develop their internal energy by practicing various breathing exercises. Chinese senior citizens, who regularly practice exercises that develop the body's internal energy, do not age as dramatically as their Western counterparts. It is often difficult to distinguish between those who are forty and those who are sixty. White hair, wrinkled skin, and a stiffening gait can be delayed and in some instances completely avoided by such internal exercise.

According to traditional Chinese medicine, the human body's functioning is supported by a vital energy called *ch'i*, which flows through a series of channels that roughly correspond to the circulatory and nervous systems. A baby is born with a tremendous amount of *ch'i*, and this allows it to gain an ounce a day. But as we age, the amount of energy within the body begins to decline. According to the Chinese, the condition of one's *ch'i* determines the physical condition of the body. A strong, vigorous person has strong *ch'i*.

It is important to note that *ch'i* is not a mysterious force affecting the body, like the ether of the medieval alchemists. From a Western perspective, *ch'i* can be viewed as the amount of oxygen that is pumped throughout the body by the respiratory process. Whether it is called cardiovascular fitness, aerobic health, or good *ch'i*, both Eastern and Western medicine acknowledge that regulating the breathing process can affect the physical health of an individual for the better. From another angle, the U.S. Surgeon General has demonstrated the adverse consequences of inhibiting proper lung function through habits such as smoking, the number one preventable cause of early death.

In China, the *Yellow Emperor's Classic of Internal Medicine* (*Nei-ching*) is considered to be the foundation of all later medical theory. First recorded more than two thousand years ago, the book notes that people can remain healthy by practicing deep breathing to allow the smooth flow of the *ch'i* throughout the body. Another classic, the *Guangzi* (c. 300 B.C.E), points out that "the practice of breathing will help improve the function of the eyes and ears and the general fitness of the four limbs, and this will in turn accumulate abundant energy and vigor in the body."

Proper breathing in a relaxed state increases awareness because of the increased oxygen flow to the brain and throughout the body. The concept of *ch'i* and the breathing exercises that facilitate its development are an aspect of Chinese culture that has been largely overlooked by Western scholars. Even today, it is estimated that fifteen million people in mainland China practice *ch'i* exercises daily.

The foundation of the later breathing schools—including I Chuan—is the cosmological framework of Taoism. Taoist cosmology is based on the idea that the human being is a microcosmic reflection of the macrocosmic universe. Thus, the workings of the body correspond to the natural processes of the earth and heavens.

The human body and its internal organs are viewed as possessing natural structures that have cosmic analogies. The earliest Taoist text based on these analogies is a work of the second century B.C.E. known as the *Huai-nan-tzu*. The book is based on the concept that one can achieve an integration of self with the natural world through meditative breathing. It says:

> What is spiritual is received from Heaven while the body and its material form are derived from the Earth. It is the harmony of the spirits of yin and yang on which all harmony depends. . . .
>
> Heaven has four seasons, five elements, nine divisions, three hundred and sixty days. Similarly, man has four limbs, five internal organs, nine orifices and three hundred and sixty joints. Heaven has wind, rain, cold, heat; man similarly, has joy, anger, taking, giving. . . . Man forms a trinity with Heaven and Earth, and his mind is the master. . . .

The concept of the trinity of heaven, earth, and man has had a great influence on Chinese philosophy. Viewing the human being as a microcosmic universe, the early Taoists attempted to achieve a harmony of body and mind through breathing exercises. The development of the *ch'i* within the body was a way to fully balance and integrate the universe within with the universe outside.

Lao-tzu asks in the *Tao Te Ching*: "Can you concentrate on your breathing to reach harmony and become as an innocent babe?" A baby is born breathing naturally, with the entire body. As a child grows, the breathing process becomes more localized and gradually moves upward. Most adults breathe from their upper chests, greatly reducing the maximum amount of oxygen they can take into their bodies. This is exactly what Chuang-tzu means when he writes: "The perfect man breathes through his heels, while the ordinary man breathes through his throat." Later, he goes on to state:

Concentrate on the goal of meditation.
Do not listen with your ear, but listen with your mind;
Not with your mind, but with your breath.

Let the hearing stop with your ear,
Let the mind stop with its images.
Breathing means to empty oneself and to wait for Tao.

In this context, a reasonable translation of the term *Tao* would be "the way of realization and inner peace"—an idea related to the Buddhist concept of enlightenment. The attainment of Tao can be regarded as the most important theme in Chinese philosophy.

In ancient China the most famed physicians were not those who healed the sick but those who ensured the continued health and longevity of their patients. Curing someone who was already sick was compared to digging a well long after you had become thirsty. Following this tradition, the practice of I Chuan aims at the development and maintenance of good health.

The theory of I Chuan derives from the principles of longevity first outlined by the Taoist sages more than two thousand years ago. The goal is to harmonize and cultivate the body's energy to prevent the onset of disease and slow down the aging process. In short, the Tao of I Chuan is the way to ensure a long and healthy life.

MASTER WANG AND THE ORIGIN OF I CHUAN

The founder of I Chuan, Grand Master Wang Xiang Zhai, was born in 1886 in Shen Xian, Hopei Province, China, the birthplace of many famous martial art masters. When he was eight years old, and sickly because of asthma, he was introduced to a friend of his father, Grand Master Guo Yun Shen. The seventy-year-old grand master was venerated among his peers as the generation's leading authority in martial arts.

Grand Master Guo took a liking to the young

boy, and after a solemn initation ceremony, he accepted Wang as his student. Though the grand master had many famous students, he was still searching for someone special who would be the heir to whom he would pass on his knowledge before he died. Wang Xiang Zhai proved to be that special student.

For six years the master treated Wang like a son, knowing that he would be a great master one day. Even when Guo was aged and bedridden, he kept Wang at his side and continued his teaching. When his master died, Wang Xiang Zhai was fourteen years old and already very well accomplished. He knew, however, that he would have to continue to improve if he was to assume the place of Grand Master Guo. With this purpose in mind, he set out to find good teachers.

In the course of his study Wang absorbed the principles of Hsing I Chuan, the soft power of T'ai Chi Chuan, and the dexterity, quickness of action, and nimbleness of Pa Kua Chuan—the three major internal martial art styles. He also learned the practice of standing meditation, which originated in the Shaolin temple founded by Bodhidharma, the first patriarch of Ch'an (or Zen) Buddhism in China. Bringing all these influences together, the I Chuan practice of Master Wang is perhaps the highest form of Chinese internal energy development.

A poem by Master Wang illustrates the theoretical sources of I Chuan:

Action obeys the mind.
Nothingness brings peace to the mind's movement.
Pugilism by origin has no technique;
If action has some technique it remains nothingness.
One skill is untenable;
The absence of technique contains them all.
Let power come and be used naturally,
It refines a person's spirit.

Using your heart, breathe out and in,
Learn and understand its function.
Do not be very close to it nor very distant,
Rather hold the key and be the pivot.
Although this action is without form, it can change
itself from time to time and manifest itself as
you feel.
Draw inward the light of your eye and listen to the
inside of your body.
Train your nerves to be sensitive in all ways.

This poem reflects I Chuan's roots in ancient Taoist philosophy. These Taoist principles are expressed in the ancient book of internal medicine, the *Yellow Emperor's Classic:*

> The immortal men in ancient times could combine heaven and earth. They could contain yin and yang because they absorbed the essence of ch'i and because they could stand silently concentrating their attention.

The complementary forces of nature, *yin* and *yang*, must be kept in balance for one to achieve peace and good health. The cultivation of *ch'i* is enhanced by the standing meditation derived from the second source of I Chuan's philosophy, Ch'an Buddhism. Lines five through eight of Master Wang's poem refer to the standing meditation methods of Shaolin, a style of Chinese martial art derived from Buddhist meditative practices.

Grand Master Wang's method of training was unique. In contrast to those martial artists who practiced only the external forms, he emphasized practicing and developing internal force. To Master Wang, without the inner, mind practice, developing other skills was like putting the cart before the horse. The art of I Chuan that he created was based on the concept that one's mind controls one's form.

I Chuan combines the essential parts of every style of martial art. That is why it is also called Da Chen Chuan, or "Great Achievement Pugilism." The source of its power is the secret training methods of standing meditation. Masters have generally been reluctant to offer their prized exercises to the public, teaching them only to one or two favorite students. Grand Master Wang offered the essential principles and forms of I Chuan to all his students, and they have continued to transmit this rare art to this day.

PRINCIPLES OF I CHUAN PRACTICE

I Chuan makes use of the natural mind-body connection in a way that distinguishes it from most other forms of exercise. In both Western sports and Eastern external martial arts, the individual is constantly striving to perform better: to run faster, to do more situps, to stretch further, to punch harder. The mind is making demands upon the body that the body cannot fulfill, and the body must strain and adapt to meet those demands. This is a method of training that works for many people, but the results are limited to increasing bodily strength. Furthermore, the relationship it establishes between mind and body is one of master and slave—the mind whipping the body to ever greater accomplishments.

I Chuan practice is entirely different. The exercises are soft, slow, and gentle, involving a minimum of physical effort while requiring significant mental effort: concentration, directed attention, patience, persistence, imagination, and visualization. The mind does more and the body does less than in external exercise, and the result is that a kind of surplus energy builds up in the body, just as money accrues in a bank account when one deposits more than one withdraws.

Many athletes and dancers mentally rehearse their performance, visualizing each action perfectly many times before actually moving the body. In I Chuan, one does the mental work *while* the body is moving slowly and softly, thus ensuring that the psychic surplus goes into the body itself. The quality of this new mind-body relationship will become immediately apparent after only a few practice sessions.

All the I Chuan exercises entail an energy connection to the earth through the soles of the feet (a primary acupuncture point, also known as the "bubbling spring well"), which is enhanced by the pumping action of the initial exercise and distributed throughout the body in a variety of patterns or circuits. Although people's experiences with the exercises will vary—since each person's characteristic energy patterns and areas of strength and weakness are unique—the sensation of a firm, rooted connection to the ground, like that of a tree or healthy plant, is almost universal. This experience is a powerful counterbalance to the top-heavy energy pattern of most people in Western society, particularly those who do sedentary mental work and do not walk or exercise their lower body for most of the day.

I Chuan practice also causes one's breathing to drop from the upper chest to the *tan-t'ien*, a major energy center located approximately two to three inches below the navel. This deep breathing provides the body with more oxygen and develops more *ch'i*. Ultimately the I Chuan practitioner breathes with the entire body. (More will be said about this later.)

WHERE, WHEN, AND HOW TO PRACTICE

To begin with, wear loose, comfortable clothes that do not bind the body or constrict breathing. Soft, flat-soled shoes with plenty of traction are best. Bare-foot practice is recommended only for those with strong feet and ankles and is preferably done only on a natural surface, such as sand, grass, or earth. Avoid Chinese Kung Fu shoes with plastic soles—they are too slippery.

The location of practice must be carefully selected. It should be quiet, peaceful, and free from distracting sights or noises. One becomes quite sensitive to external movement during I Chuan practice and will notice even a slight draft through an open door or window. Outdoor practice is best, but it is recommended only in natural surroundings and is not to be done in wind, rain, snow, or extreme heat or cold. The body works hardest in the hottest and coldest weather. Because circulation is best in the summer, summer practice is the most beneficial. Spring is better than fall, and fall is better than winter.

Early morning, before the demands of the day begin, is the optimal practice time. But midday, around sunset, or even midnight can be a productive practice time if the environment is good and you are able to clear the mind of worries and distractions. If your schedule is tight, practice whenever you have free time. You should feel rested before beginning practice (a brief nap can be helpful) and you should avoid extreme activity immediately afterward.

Practice before you eat, or wait at least an hour and a half after eating. Drink a cup of warm water before starting. This is good for your circulation and can help stimulate the internal force. Avoid drinking anything cold an hour before and an hour after practicing. When you do this exercise, your body becomes like an oven, and the shock of coldness can be detrimental. Don't practice in an air-conditioned room or use a fan to cool yourself off afterward—as with drinking cold water, these will use up the energy you generate just keeping the body warm.

No special diet is necessary when practicing I Chuan. Eat what you know is good for you and be moderate. There are no special requirements regarding sexual activity, either. Be moderate and do what feels natural. I Chuan practice should not be done for several hours before or after sexual relations.

You will need thirty minutes to an hour for your practice. Be sure to have enough time so you will not have to rush through the exercises or meditation. Consistency is important. It is better to practice thirty minutes a day every day than to miss sessions and try to make them up through longer practices. In the beginning, a half-hour a day, including the warmup exercise, is long enough.

There are three mistakes to avoid. First, don't overdo any of the exercises. Second, don't use too much physical force while practicing. Third, don't hold your breath or breathe unnaturally. Any of these mistakes will impede the flow of *ch'i* through your body. If your chest feels tight and congested and you feel out of breath, if you feel dizzy, or if you perspire too much and feel nauseated, then you are overdoing it. Rest and you will feel better.

I Chuan will gradually become part of your daily routine, like brushing your teeth or eating breakfast. The benefits of such consistent effort are immeasurable.

GUIDELINES FOR PRACTICE

1. Move slowly and smoothly. Move as if you were underwater, feeling the air as a medium, not just empty space. Make no sudden stops or starts, no jerky or awkward movement. Maintain an even, uniform rhythm. Beginners often move too quickly, and so they must strive to go ever more slowly and smoothly. I Chuan has no hard edges. Every action—including changes of direction—should be rounded or slightly curved.

2. *Exert no muscular force.* When first attempting the I Chuan movements, many beginners, especially those who have trained in Karate or other hard-style martial arts, tense their hands, forearms, upper arms, leg muscles, stomach muscles, and so forth. This is counterproductive, as the muscular tension only interferes with the development of internal force. While standing erect and performing the movements, you should relax the muscles as much as possible. *Think* the movements. They will then take on a soft, gentle quality, which is the perfect condition for the flow of *ch'i* and the development of inner force.

3. *Maintain correct body posture.* Stand with your feet parallel, shoulder width apart. The toes may point slightly outward, though no more than 45 degrees. The knees should be directly over the feet. Pay particular attention to the foot alignment if you have weak arches or other foot or ankle problems. You should feel a slight cupping or gripping sensation under the center of the foot, although the foot muscles should not be strongly tensed.

Do not allow the buttocks to stick out. The back should be as straight as possible, but do not tense the muscles. Drop the shoulders and elbows, and let them remain that way, with no excess tension in the shoulder and neck muscles.

Look straight ahead at eye level (except when slightly turning the head), with the chin parallel to the ground and the eyes half open and not focused on any particular object. You should feel rooted and relaxed.

4. *Let the mind be calm and quiet.* When practic-

ing I Chuan, you should be relaxed, peaceful, serene, and confident. Do not rush the exercises; do not worry about whether you are doing them exactly right; do not allow yourself to think anxious or distracting thoughts. Rather, focus your mind gently on the movements, feeling the air with your hands, feeling your roots connecting you to the earth. While doing I Chuan, let it be the most important thing in the world. No problems or demands on your attention should intrude on your practice. With time and steady, persistent practice, you will attain a state of relaxed concentration.

5. *Breathe naturally.* Unlike most martial arts and *ch'i* development practices, I Chuan does not call for coordinating the movements with the breath. Breathe naturally, at whatever rhythm feels most comfortable. Over time, your breathing will become deeper, slower, and quieter, but do not force this to happen. Keep the mouth closed, the tongue against the palate, and breathe through the nose (unless your nose is stuffed). If you have been accustomed to exhaling during pressing or pushing actions (as in most exercise systems and martial arts), you will soon be fascinated to feel your breath interacting with the movements in a far greater variety of combinations. Sometimes you will exhale as you lift the arms and inhale as you press them. Sometimes you will breathe in and out several times through a single movement. This may feel strange at first, but it will soon become quite natural.

FOCUSING THE MIND

As mentioned earlier, the mental aspects of I Chuan are as important as, if not more important than, the physical actions. Focusing your attention on the proper thoughts during practice will help you to remain alert, relaxed, and serene. The following are all good ways to achieve this mental focus.

- Maintain a pleasant expression on your face, and evoke the feeling that comes just as you are about to smile. Then slowly and in sequence, relax the head, neck, shoulders, arms, back, chest, stomach, legs, and feet.

- Listen to the sounds nearest you, then to those farther away, then to those farther still. Listen from inside to outside, from the loudest sounds to faintest.

- Imagine yourself floating in a warm river, with water flowing all around you.

- Imagine you are taking a hot shower. Hear the sound of the water around your feet. Feel the warmth on your body.

- Feel as if you are standing in a warm sea, your lower body submerged. Next, imagine that the water is up to your chest, flowing directly against your body, its force gently rocking you. Let yourself sway naturally.

- Feel as if you are a tall, old tree. Your feet are roots reaching deep down into the earth. Nothing could possibly knock you over.

- Imagine you are walking in ankle-deep, warm, soft mud. It has resistance, but you can move through it easily.

- Feel your feet lightly trampling on a giant piece of fluffy cotton. Let your body sway slightly from side to side.

- Feel the backs of your shoulders, your back, and your calves weightlessly leaning on air. Keep your knees slightly bent.

- Imagine that you are hanging by your hair from a tree branch. It doesn't hurt—it feels good. Imagine that your hair is being pulled very straight by the weight of your body as it hangs straight down from the tree.

- Feel as if your arms are directly out in front of you, your fingertips on top of a big balloon rising under them. Your whole body feels light and comfortable.

- If other thoughts enter your mind, just let them exit. Let them pass through. Your whole body, like an oven, melts them away.
- Think of the most beautiful places you've ever seen: the ocean, the seashore, the moon, a forest in the rain. Feel relaxed and happy.
- Imagine being in a beautiful and comfortable place, fresh air surrounding you. You are transformed into the wonderful fresh air itself and fly away, selfless and oblivious to your own body.
- Listen intently to a soft, gentle, drizzling rain. As you take in the gentle sound with rapt attention, you feel as though you could do it for a long time.

After a while, you will become very familiar with the feeling of relaxation in the body and will be able to direct it to and concentrate it in particular parts of your body. Once you do this, the relaxation will disperse throughout the rest of the body, leaving you feeling completely at ease.

At any time, you can mentally search your body for any area that is not relaxed. If you find one, "look" at it with your mind and feel the area relaxing. Do this process several times and your entire body will feel comfortable.

PART TWO
Beginner's Exercises

The following twelve exercises constitute the first level of I Chuan. With diligent practice these exercises will help you develop a free flow of *ch'i* and strengthen the body's tendons and ligaments. These developments are essential for progressing to the more advanced practices, which are outlined later in this book. Even when you begin the more advanced exercises, you will still find these exercises relaxing and beneficial and will want to incorporate some, if not all, of them into your daily routine.

Calligraphy: Create ch'i

EXERCISE 1

Flood Dragon Emerges from the Water

DESCRIPTION   The hands circle in front of the body in coordination with the bending and straightening of the legs.

1.   Extend the hands away from the body, with elbows slightly bent and palms facing outward. The fingers are gently extended, but the hands are not stiff or tense. As you sink the body down by bending your knees, slowly lower the hands in a smooth arc. *Note:* Do not change the alignment of your feet as you sink. Make sure that your knees are pointing directly over the toes. (Figs. 1–4)

1

2

3

4

5

6

2. Bend the knees to approximately a 45-degree angle as you continue the arc of the hands in front of the thighs, palms now facing down. Keep the back straight, but avoid tucking in the buttocks. When the hands reach the centerline of the body, cross the palms without touching, right palm under left, and begin to arc upward. (Figs. 5–6)

7

3. Slowly straighten the knees and raise the body vertically. The hands continue to circle, rising in front of the body until the palms face outward with the fingers pointing up at approximately face level. At this point, your legs are straight, although your knees should not be locked. (Figs. 7–8)

8

4. Let the hands float out and down again as you begin to bend the knees and sink the body downward once more. (Fig. 9) Repeat the exercise 20 times.

9

Points to Remember

- Keep shoulders down, arms soft, not tense. Feel the air with your palms and fingertips.
- As you bend your knees, feel yourself becoming more and more rooted to the ground. Keep this connection as you come up.
- Keep perfect vertical alignment. Don't allow your body to tilt forward or backward as you move up and down.
- Relax. Don't push. Smile inwardly. Once you have acquired the proper form of the exercise, allow it to happen almost by itself.

EXERCISE 2

Heaven and Earth Sink and Float

DESCRIPTION   The palms rise and fall as the body stays rooted.

10

1. Straighten the legs, just short of locking the knees. Raise the hands to shoulder level, palms facing down. *Slowly* press the palms down. Without tensing the muscles, imagine that you are pushing a large ball down into the water (or create some other image of moderate resistance). (Figs. 10–12)

2. When the hands reach a point just below the waist, slowly turn them around so that the palms face upward. (Figs. 13–14)

11

3. Slowly raise the palms upward to just below shoulder height, again evoking an image of moderate resistance, such as lifting a medicine ball or raising the hands through a thick liquid. (Fig. 15)

4. Softly turn the palms over to face downward. (Figs. 16–17) Repeat the exercise 20 times.

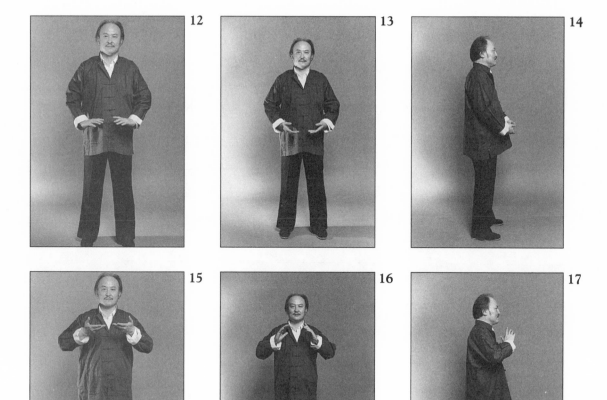

Points to Remember

- The transitions between up and down are important. Make them gradual, curved, and conscious, so that you do not lose the feeling in your palms as you turn them over.
- Relax the shoulders, arms, and hands, eliminating all unnecessary tension. Apply energy only through your imagination, and do not tense your muscles.
- Breathe naturally, and do not try to coordinate your breath with the movements.
- Keep a feeling of rootedness and energy in your feet and legs; don't let all your attention shift to your hands. The exercise is of no value if your energy connection to the earth is not maintained.

EXERCISE 3
Two Baby Swallows Flying

DESCRIPTION   The hands rise and extend to the sides, like birds flying in opposite directions.

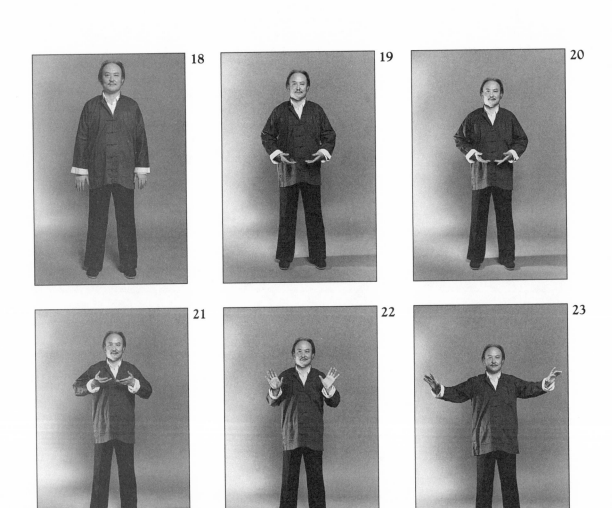

1. As in the previous exercise, the legs are straight but not stiff. Raise the palms slowly from waist level to chest height. (Figs. 18–21)

2. Slowly rotate the hands so that the fingers point up and then out to the sides. (Fig. 22)

3. Gently push the hands out and to the side, fingers leading, until the arms are extended three-quarters at waist level. (Figs. 23–24)

4. Bring the hands inward in front of the *tan-t'ien* (2–3 inches below the navel), and turn the palms upward. (Fig. 25) Repeat the exercise 20 times.

24

25

Points to Remember

- Don't overextend the arms. The movement is gentle.
- Try to feel the air as a medium through which you are gently pushing your fingers and palms.
- Breathe naturally, and do not try to coordinate your breath with the movements.
- Maintain some awareness in your legs, feet, and trunk so you sustain the quality of being rooted to the ground.

EXERCISE 4
Pick a Star from the Pleiades

DESCRIPTION   The arms alternate, as if running in slow motion.

1. The legs are straight but not stiff. Starting with arms down and hands at your sides, slowly raise the left hand in front of your body at about a 45-degree angle from the body's centerline. Turn your body slightly to the left (the trunk movement emanating from the *tan-t'ien*) so that you are looking at your palm. The elbow remains as low as possible while the hand rises to slightly above shoulder level. At the same time, bring the right hand backward, just behind the right buttock, and close the fingers into a "baby fist," with the thumb inside the other fingers. Close this hand gently, without tensing the arm muscles. (Figs. 26–29)

2. Allow the left hand to glide downward as the right hand uncurls from the fist and rises in front of the body, reaching a point just below shoulder level and 45 degrees from center. The whole body turns, moving as one unit, until you are looking at the right palm. The left hand curls into a baby fist behind the left buttock. You are now in a mirror image of the previous position. (Figs. 30–31)

3. Repeat the exercise 10 times on each side.

Points to Remember
- Move slowly and smoothly, maintaining a relaxed feeling.
- Turn the body only slightly—just enough to look at your extended hand. The feet should not move.
- Breathe naturally, at whatever rate is most comfortable.

EXERCISE 5

Stand on the Earth and Hold the Heavens

DESCRIPTION The palms rise slowly and press gently upward.

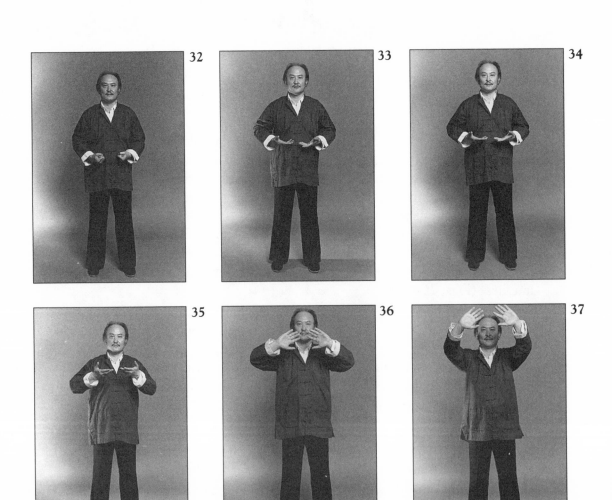

1. Start with legs straight but not locked, the hands in lightly closed fists just above the hips. Slowly open the hands and lift the palms in front of the body, gradually turning the palms toward you as they rise above shoulder height. (Figs. 32–35)

2. When the palms are at face level, rotate the hands so that they face outward and then upward. At the same time, raise the eyes and head slightly to look skyward, past the hands. Sense a subtle feeling of pushing upward. Do not extend the arms fully, and raise the hands no higher than the top of the head. (Figs. 36–38)

3. Gently and slowly lower the hands, rotating palms toward the body, lowering the eyes to look straight ahead.

4. Bring hands to rest, in lightly closed fists, at waist level. (Fig. 39) Repeat 20 times.

38

39

Points to Remember

- The physical movement is small and gentle. You may extend mentally upward through the palms, but keep the actual pushing motion very slight.

- The opening and closing position feels stable and rooted. Try to keep this heavy quality even as you lift your arms. Do not allow your rootedness to diminish as you raise your hands.

- As the arms sink down, do not let the back collapse, but keep the spine straight. Try to have an upward feeling in your spine, as though it were attached to a cord suspended from above.

EXERCISE 6

Pull the Ox Tail Back

DESCRIPTION   Step forward and raise fist.

40

41

42

1. From a natural standing posture, step gently forward onto the left foot. As your weight shifts onto the forward leg (to approximately 70 percent of the weight), slowly raise the left fist in front of your body to the level of your chin. The arms should be only about 50–60 percent extended. At the same time, draw your right fist backward to a point a few inches behind the right hip. Pause for a moment. (Figs. 40–42)

2. Moving slowly and with good balance, step back to the starting position as you gradually drop your hands. (Fig. 43)

3. Step forward onto the right foot, raising the right fist and drawing the left fist back behind your hip—the exact mirror image of the first movement. (Figs. 44–45)

4. Step back and lower the hands. Repeat 10 times on each side.

Points to Remember

- Step softly and gently, gradually shifting the weight to the front foot. The body remains erect and balanced throughout the step.
- Do not tense the arms or clench the fists tight; rather, strive for a feeling of extending energy through the fists in both forward and backward directions.
- Look beyond the extended fist, and keep the back straight.

EXERCISE 7

Spring Silkworms Spin Silk

DESCRIPTION   The hands thrust forward, then pull back as if drawing silk from a cocoon.

46

47

48

1. Stand with the legs straight and the knees unlocked. Bring the hands up to lower chest level, with the fingers extended forward. Slowly extend the arms forward as if pushing your fingertips through a thick medium. Stop when your arms are 70–75 percent extended. (Figs. 46–48)

2. Bring the thumb and forefingers of each hand together as if grasping something light and delicate. Slowly and continuously, draw the hands backward, as if pulling silk from a cocoon. (Figs. 49–51)

3. Pause when hands are just in front of chest. (Fig. 52) Repeat 20 times.

Point to Remember

• The movement should be slow, steady, and continuous, without jerks or breaks.

EXERCISE 8
Push Two Horses Back

DESCRIPTION   The palms push backward and circle beside the hips.

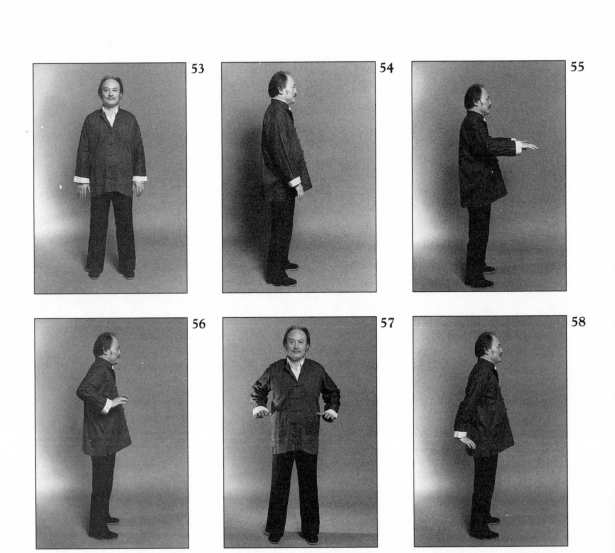

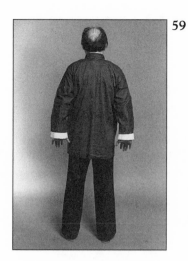 59

 60

 61

 62

1. Stand with the legs straight but not stiff. Slowly bend the elbows, drawing the hands up to hip level on either side of the body. Gently press the palms backward, until they just pass the body line. (Figs. 53–59)

2. Draw the hands back in a circle toward the front, allowing the wrists to lead the motion of the hands. (Figs. 60–62) Repeat 20 times.

Points to Remember

- The hands should be relaxed and soft, yet feel as if they are moving through warm, heavy liquid.
- Do not allow the shoulder muscles to tense up. Stay relaxed.
- Breathe naturally and easily.

EXERCISE 9

Two Hands Grasp Emptiness

DESCRIPTION   The hands open and close in front of the body.

1.   Stand with the legs straight but not stiff. Raise the hands to shoulder height, slightly in front of the body. Slowly close the fingers into a light fist. (Figs. 63–65)

2.   Slowly open the fingers until they are extended but not fully straightened. Close and open again 20 times. (Figs. 66–67)

63

64

65

 66  67

Point to Remember

- The more slowly and evenly the hands open and close, the better. Avoid sudden, jerky movements, and do not clench the fists too tight.

EXERCISE 10
Small T'ai Chi Circle

DESCRIPTION   The palms circle in front of the body.

74

75

76

1. Stand with the legs straight but not stiff. Slowly bring the palms up in front of the body, as if holding a large barrel in front of the waist. (Figs. 68–70)

2. Bring the hands toward the body, palms turning down. Then press the palms down along the body, curving them outward when they reach the level of the navel. (Figs. 71–75)

3. Curve palms toward the body as you raise them again (as in step 1). (Fig. 76) Repeat the cycle 20 times.

Points to Remember

- The movement is continuous and circular, without stops or accelerations.
- The imaginary circle described by the hands includes part of your own torso.

EXERCISE 11

Circling Left and Right

DESCRIPTION   The torso circles clockwise and counterclockwise.

77

78

79

80

81

82

83

1. Stand with the legs straight but not stiff. Place the palms on the lower back and rub several times, until warmth is felt in the lumbar region. (Fig. 77)

2. Slowly circle the head and torso in a clockwise direction, keeping the feet firmly planted and the eyes open. You may bend fairly far forward and to the sides, but lean only very slightly backward. (Figs. 78–83) Repeat 10 times.

3. Pause, then circle in the counterclockwise direction 10 times.

Points to Remember

- Keep your weight centered, and do not allow it to shift around as your head and torso move.
- Stay relaxed, and keep your breathing easy and natural. Don't tense or tighten up at any point in the circle.

EXERCISE 12

Open and Close the Tan-T'ien

DESCRIPTION   The hands spread apart and come together in front of the *tan-t'ien*.

89

1. Stand as in the previous exercises. Bring the hands up in front of the body, just below navel height. Slowly separate the hands, pulling the fingers outward in opposite directions, as if you were pulling open a pair of Oriental screen doors. (Figs. 84–85)

2. When the hands are just past the body line, gradually turn the palms toward each other and bring the hands together in front of the *tan-t'ien*. (Figs. 86–88)

3. Stop when the hands are about 6 inches apart, turn palms outward, and repeat. (Fig. 89) Repeat 20 times.

Point to Remember
   • Stay relaxed. Don't let your shoulders rise.

PART THREE
Advanced Exercises

Calligraphy: When standing, focus the mind.

I Chuan and Taoist Alchemy

Part Two presented the beginning I Chuan exercises, which are designed to create a free flow of *ch'i* within the body. This is the first stage of I Chuan practice. To achieve the higher stages, which involve enhanced *ch'i* production and ultimately the attainment of higher levels of consciousness, one must practice sitting and standing meditation postures. These postures are perhaps the most effective means of developing *ch'i* and are also extremely powerful tools in focusing the mind and shifting consciousness.

The advanced exercises are rooted in the theories of the Inner Elixir school. This school of Taoist alchemy, which became widespread during the Sung dynasty, was concerned with the development of physical and spiritual immortality—a pursuit that has been an integral part of high culture in China since ancient times. Various terms have been used to describe the attainment of immortality, referring either to a level of consciousness that does not disintegrate after death or to a physical body that does not perish, gradually becoming less and less material over hundreds of years, until it is completely transmuted into an eternal body of light.

The Taoist alchemists sought immortality by cultivating intrinsic energy. The *tan-t'ien* is the reservoir of the *ch'i*, and when the *ch'i* overflows, it is said to permeate the bones. All aging is said to cease when human energy becomes one with the energy of the universe. As the vital principle of the nervous system, *ch'i* circulates through the body in a perpetual current that flows, in regular cycles, between the opposite poles of *yin* and *yang*. When properly channeled and concentrated, *ch'i* can become an enormous source of strength. In I Chuan, this is referred to as internal power.

Simplified, the Taoist alchemical formula is as follows:

Sexual energy is turned into ch'i (vital energy).
Ch'i is further refined into spirit (willful consciousness).
Spirit is transformed into emptiness.
Through emptiness, the individual becomes eternally
one with the Tao (the supreme way of nature).

This formula lies at the heart of the ancient Chinese mystery tradition of immortality and of I Chuan. It contains a number of concepts that must be clarified. The reader should be aware, however, that the explanations are an attempt to describe a higher state of consciousness that is, by its nature, indescribable. The habitual thought patterns created through language are, in fact, considered one of the chief impediments to higher consciousness.

The principles of the Inner Elixir school were first outlined in written form in a second-century work by Wei P'o-yang entitled *Chou-i Ts'an-t'ung-ch'i* or "Meditation on Identity and Unity." This text became famous as the source for commentaries by Chu Hsi and Yü Yen in the twelfth and thirteenth centuries, respectively. These authors describe a theory that is fundamental to the internal martial arts. It asserts that the "elixir" which promotes longevity is composed of three precious substances—*ching* ("essence," sexual energy), *ch'i* (breath, vital energy), and *shen* (spirit). Each of these substances has a twofold nature and functions on an individual level in people and on a cosmic level within the universe.

Ching is manifested in its material form as reproductive fluids. Within individuals, *ching* is sexual energy, which maintains the life and vitality of the human body. On a cosmic level, *ching* is the life energy of heaven and earth, which causes the light of the sun and moon and growth and fertility in nature. *Ching* is similar to the Hindu concept of *kundalini,* and in both Chinese and Indian texts, the base of the spine is its place of abode within the human body. When awakened, it manifests its power.

Ch'i, translated as "breath" or "vital energy," is of paramount importance in the soft martial arts because it is the source of all internal power. At its highest level, *ch'i* can create tremendous force without muscular exertion. This energy is cultivated by breathing techniques and is created by the refinement of the *ching.* In the internal arts, one attempts to breathe as smoothly and naturally as an infant. The Inner Elixir school calls this "embryonic breathing," and it is in keeping with the Taoist tradition first recorded in the *Tao Te Ching* and the writings of Chuang-tzu. On a cosmic level, *ch'i* is the energy behind heaven and earth that provides the impetus for perpetual change.

Shen, or spirit, is difficult to translate. It seems to refer to both *shih shen* (ordinary consciousness) and *yüan shen* (spiritual consciousness.) *Shih shen* is composed of all mental processes that are acquired during or after birth, such as the sense of self, thoughts, feelings, and the senses. *Yüan shen* is the spiritual consciousness, which exists before birth. As a person ages, this "original mind" is more and more obscured by ordinary consciousness. The cultivation of the inner elixir is an attempt to reverse this process through meditative techniques. The sage is one who has "returned to the source"—that is, to prebirth consciousness. On a cosmic level, *yüan shen* involves the union of the individual with the Tao, the spiritual consciousness of heaven and earth, the original mind of nature manifested as life energy.

The basic formula common to both Taoist philosophy and the martial tradition is the following:

Through compounding sexual energy (*ching*), the breath (*ch'i*) is transformed; through compounding the breath, the spirit (shen) is transformed. Thus, ching, ch'i, and shen are the most fundamental elements in the process of meditative breathing.

The refinement of shen is ultimately a return to emptiness (hsü), which is associated with the state of a human being before birth. After birth, hsü has two aspects: ming (life or destiny) and hsing (spiritual consciousness). Ming is the human lifespan, which steadily deteriorates after birth. Hsing is the root of spiritual consciousness.

The goal in I Chuan is to fuse the material ming with the spiritual hsing, and by doing so, to return to the original, perpetual, and all-encompassing state of void. As Lao-tzu says of the sage, "He never deviates from his real nature and thus returns to the innocence of the infant."

The concept of a higher permanent state of consciousness has been described in many different terms throughout China's history, before and after the arrival of Buddhism. Some of these terms include: emptiness (shunyata), void, enlightenment, original mind, prenatal consciousness, attainment of Tao, awakening (bodhi), returning to the source, and bud-dhahood. All of these words refer to an experience that is beyond language. The essential idea is that before birth every human being has a pure, pristine, untarnished state of enlightened consciousness, without the false constructs of self and other. After birth, a child learns to perceive in terms of the language and norms imposed by culture. This socialization process obscures the original, innate purity of perception.

By relaxing the mind into its own natural state, the I Chuan practitioner strives to regain the mind's original, self-existing pristine awareness. This aware-ness is the essential unchanging ground from which all things arise. In the Tao Te Ching, Lao-tzu offers a concrete analogy, saying that a room is not a room without the space (emptiness) between the four walls, which provides a chamber with its form. In Buddhism, this is expressed in the notion that form is emptiness and emptiness is form.

The above description of the psychology of internal alchemy is not adequate by itself, because the spiritual evolution of the mind cannot occur without the simultaneous physical evolution of what is called *ch'i* in Chinese, *prana* in Sanskrit, and *lung* in Tibetan—that is, the innate energy of the body. Spiritual awakening cannot occur until a free flow of energy throughout the body has been achieved by greatly increasing the *ch'i*.

Breathing is the physical process that unites the body and mind and develops and causes the *ch'i* to circulate freely throughout the energy centers of the body. It is the source of all life. The I Chuan method of breathing, combined with standing meditation, is the safest and fastest method of developing and circulating this tremendous energy, which lies dormant within the human body at the base of the spine, and which is the source of all higher consciousness. I Chuan balances the flow of *ch'i* and returns the mind to its original consciousness. It does this safely and at the body's own pace through natural, unforced breathing and through harmony with coexisting energies in nature.

When a fetus is within the womb, it breathes from its lower abdomen through the umbilical cord. With birth, the infant is forced to use its lungs, but it still uses its lower abdomen to breathe. The newborn's consciousness is pristine and untarnished by conceptual thought, and its *ch'i* is fully active and freely circulating, which allows rapid growth and physical development. But as the child grows, conceptual thought patterns are imposed by language, and breathing becomes further and further removed from the abdomen. By adulthood, the original consciousness is completely obscured, the person breathes from the chest area, and the small amount of *ch'i* that is produced by such shallow, unnatural breathing is rapidly depleted in routine sexual activity.

I Chuan reverses this scenario. The standing meditation postures cause breathing patterns to gradually revert to the lower abdomen. All advanced I Chuan practitioners have sunk their breathing in this way, which means that every breath produces *ch'i*, and this develops tremendous physical energy and vitality. The classical idea that sums up the ancient alchemical premise of I Chuan is that the only real elixir of immortality is your own *ch'i*.

PRINCIPLES OF STANDING MEDITATION

I Chuan is deceptively simple. When practicing it, one appears merely to be breathing. A sapling, no matter how soft and pliant, remains still and upright, and yet it is constantly growing to become a tall and strong tree. Just as the growth of a tree is difficult to perceive, our own inner growth is often not apparent. This is the inspiration for *chan chuang*, the standing meditation practice that is an important part of I Chuan.

The human body's metabolic resistance to illness and disease, determines whether one will grow healthy or weak. Like trees people grow in accord with their innate characteristics and their surrounding environment. *Chan chuang* enhances and reinforces the metabolism, rendering it healthier.

While practicing, one's outward appearance remains peaceful as the internal force develops and the fire of life is lit. The activity is total, affecting every organ, bone and tissue. The practice stimulates blood circulation and removes circulatory blocks, and it relaxes and refines the nervous system. During practice, *ch'i* is created, which stimulates the autonomic nervous system. Blood flow is optimal during practice, and afterward red and white blood corpuscles and hemoglobin content increase, thereby supplying more oxygen to the entire system. *Chan chuang*'s revitalizing and refreshing effects are experienced as greater energy and clarity of mind, which are reflected in the facial features of the practitioner.

To cultivate internal force, one must be relaxed and assume a natural posture. The mind is focused, and the whole body becomes unified in its movements. Second, while the mind is expanding, it can make use of the inexhaustible wisdom and power of the natural world. In *Chan Chuang*, Master Wang combined Buddhist and Taoist ideas, teaching that one must have a good foundation in relaxing the body through focusing the mind. The mind's power is then one's own. This is expressed by an old Chinese saying:

> *Still as a mountain,*
> *Powerful as thunder.*

The following advanced meditation exercises may at first cause unusual muscle strain, as you use new muscles to perform new sustained exercises. Remember to go slowly. The amount of time you spend on these exercises should be built up gradually, minute by minute. (It is best to use a timer.) Over time, these exercises will become easier. With regular practice, the results of the meditations described below will soon be noticeable.

Sitting Meditation

90

91

92

93

94

95

96

97

98

99

100

101

102

1. Stay calm and relaxed throughout the meditation.

2. Sit on the edge of an armless chair with the buttocks and legs supporting your weight. Your back should not touch the chair. Plant your feet firmly on the floor, shoulder width apart, knees bent at a 90-degree angle. Keep your shoulders and elbows down throughout the meditation. Rest the hands, palms down, on the knees. The back should be straight at the waist but slightly rounded at the shoulder and neck. (Figs. 90–91)

3. Look straight ahead, chin parallel to the ground, throughout the meditation (even when your eyes are closed).

4. Close your eyes. Visualize a beautiful scene. Practice this for 5–15 minutes (build up over time).

5. After practice, rub your hands briskly for a few seconds, then rub your hands on your face and head. (Figs. 92–97)

6. Place your palms on top of your ears, fingers pointing behind you. Tap your fingers 9 times briskly on the base of the skull (the *medulla oblongata*). (In Taoism, 9 is a magical number.) (Figs. 98–102)

Standing Meditation 1

103

104

1. Stay calm and relaxed throughout the meditation.

2. Stand straight, the feet shoulder width apart, the toes pointing between straight and outward at a 45-degree angle.

3. Look straight ahead, chin parallel to the ground, throughout the practice (even when your eyes are closed).

4. Keep the shoulders and elbows down throughout the practice.

5. Place your hands at midsection, between waistline and navel, with palms facing up, fingers spread as if holding a big volleyball, without touching the body. (Figs. 103–104)

6. Close your eyes, yet retain a forward-looking gaze.

7. Visualize a beautiful scene.

8. Practice for 3–10 minutes. (Increase time very slowly, minute by minute).

Standing Meditation 2

105

106

1. Stay calm and relaxed throughout the meditation. Keep shoulders and elbows low and relaxed, even when raising arms.

2. Look straight ahead, chin parallel to the ground, throughout the practice.

3. Stand with the left foot in front of the right. The front foot should be pointing forward, while the rear foot is pointing outward 45 degrees.

4. Keep your knees bent and place 70 percent of your weight on the rear leg, 30 percent on the front.

5. Raise your left arm so that the hand is at shoulder level. Extend the arm, but keep the elbow bent. Keep the hand open but not tense, palm facing out.

6. Move the rear hand slightly above waist level and by your side. Keep the hand open but not tense, palm facing down. (Figs. 105–106)

7. Keep the back straight (avoid leaning backward), and don't tuck in your buttocks.

8. Keep your eyes half closed. Stare straight ahead, without focusing on anything.

9. Stand for 3–10 minutes (increase your time slowly, minute by minute).

10. Repeat the exercise with the opposite stance (right leg and arm forward).

PART FOUR
Drawing Power from Nature

Calligraphy: Tao

The goal of I Chuan, the attainment of Tao, is traditionally viewed as a union of the ancient triad of heaven, earth, and the human being, both within and outside of the practitioner. This union describes a person's complete oneness with the natural world of mountains, rivers, rocks, trees, lakes, oceans, wind, rain, thunder, sun, and moon. Taoists hold that all aspects of nature are important for the correct spiritual refinement of humanity, for humans are composed of the same essential elements as the various aspects of the natural world. I Chuan is a practical way of integrating oneself with these forces of nature.

In China, the internal martial arts, along with literature and the visual arts, are heavily influenced by the beauty and power of the natural world. Taoism and Ch'an Buddhism have always emphasized a return to nature's harmony as a means of self-transcendence. In Chinese literature, the sage who is at one with the Tao lives high in the mountains and forests. An intimate relationship with nature is, like meditation, a way of attaining higher truth.

At its highest level, I Chuan is intimately linked with the concept of self-cultivation. Liberating the mind through self-cultivation enables the practitioner to develop a more intuitive consciousness—a central aspect of Taoism and Buddhism. Meditation facilitates a spontaneous interaction with nature in which the separation of subject and object is transcended. Lu Chi, a third-century Chinese scholar, wrote:

Such moments, when mind and matter hold perfect communion
And wide vistas open to regions hitherto entirely barred,
Will come with irresistible force
And go, their departure none can hinder.
Hiding, they vanish like a flash of light;
Manifest, they are like sounds arising in midair.

In other words, when mind and matter, or subject and object, are fused, the mind will be able to see through the dualistic vision of reality caused by ordinary consciousness.

There is a similar union of inner and outer realities in I Chuan. *Yin* and *yang*, the five elements (wood, earth, fire, water, gold), and the trigrams of the *I Ching*, or *Book of Changes*, actively function both inside and outside the human body. Heaven and earth are represented as the upper and lower halves of the body.

The origin of many of the principles used in I Chuan can be found in the *I Ching*, the *Tao Te Ching*, and the writings of Chuang-tzu. These texts exemplify the way that the ancients penetrated the surface of the natural world to grasp its hidden essence. Such qualities as resisting and yielding, soft and hard, male and female, strength and weakness, empty and full, were seen as basic patterns of energy, which correspond to the cycles of the natural world.

The realization of emptiness is an important aspect of spiritual emancipation in both Buddhism and Taoism. But even Confucianism stresses the importance of quiet sitting for the development of social morality. It is clear that the concept of the Tao is linked to such an altered state of consciousness. I Chuan seeks union with the Tao by physical and mental emulation of the forces of the earth, such as *yin* and *yang* and the five elements.

In general, the *I Ching* affirms the life-giving, creative nature of the Tao. Harmony between heaven, earth, and the human being can only occur through one's receptiveness and adaptability to a state of perpetual change. The concept of the Tao's alternating active and passive principles of *yin* and *yang* is central to later martial arts theory. The division of the creative process into two aspects is also found in the *Tao Te Ching*.

The Yellow Emperor's Classic of Internal Medicine, the oldest medical text in China, was written during the Han dynasty (207 B.C.E.–220 C.E.). Though it has been altered and revised many times, many of the concepts are clearly of much more ancient origin. In the chapter titled "Natural Truth in Ancient Times," the author says:

> I urge you to bring into harmony for me nature, Heaven and Tao. There must be an end and a beginning. Heaven must be in accord with the lights of the sky, the celestial bodies and their course and periods. The earth below must reflect the four seasons, the five elements, that which is precious, and that which is lowly and without value—one as well as the other. Is it not that in Winter man responds to Yin (the principle of darkness and cold)? And is it not that in Summer he responds to Yang (the principle of light and warmth)?

In pursuit of longevity, Taoists sought to rediscover purity of body and mind by breathing as naturally as a baby. Chuang-tzu writes:

> The True Man of ancient times slept without dreaming and woke without care; he ate without savoring and his breath came from deep inside. The True Man breathes with his heels; the mass of men breathe with their throats. Crushed and bound down, they gasp out their words as though they are retching. Deep in their passions and desires they are shallow in the workings of Heaven.

The Taoist breathing method uses the lower abdomen and concentrates on the *tan-t'ien*, two inches below the navel. Lao-tzu says: "When one gives undivided attention to the [vital] breath, and brings it to the utmost degree of pliancy, he can become as a tender babe."

Breathing exercises involve the combination of "inner activity" (*nei-kung*) and "outer strengthening" (*chiang-chuang-kung*). This union is regarded as the "way to the preservation of life" (*yang-sheng*). The alternating relations of *yin* and *yang* and the five elements are directly influenced by *ch'i*, which functions on both a cosmic and a personal level. All maladies stem from poor circulation of the *ch'i*, and respiratory exercises seek to develop internal energy and facilitate its circulation.

In essence, the concept of the Tao suggests a return to a fundamental union of heaven, earth, and the human being. The passive and active principles of *yin* and *yang* are not antagonistic; they are mutually complementary parts of a greater whole. Health and longevity stem from a balanced and harmonious interaction of *yin* and *yang*. The sage who could maintain their balance by flowing with the cyclical currents of perpetual change was assured of a long life and attainment of Tao.

Although I Chuan can be practiced in almost any environment, at the advanced level, the practitioner actively seeks to draw energy from the sun and moon, mountains and rivers, rocks and trees, and combines these forces with the body's own energies. The methods that follow have never been taught openly in the past. They have been treasured as secrets because of the enormous power they can unlock within an individual.

The initial changes that occur through these practices are subtle. Greater benefits come through continued effort over an extended period of time and vary according to the individual. The key is not how long one trains, but how regularly. Most people do not have the time necessary to utilize all the following techniques. If that is true for you, select the aspects of nature that you are most drawn to and that are most accessible to you.

I Chuan uses three kinds of meditation to unlock the energy centers of the human body (known as *chakras* in the Indian system): moving meditation, sitting meditation, and standing meditation. Since the following techniques are derived from the highest level of I Chuan practice, the individual should seek mainly to use the most advanced technique, standing meditation, within a natural environment. Excellent results can be achieved, however, by using sitting and moving meditation as well.

The techniques should *not* be employed by anyone who does not wish to experience serious physical, mental, and spiritual changes based on the utilization of natural, elemental forces. A gentle stream can become a raging torrent, and a summer breeze can become a tornado; all is governed by the interaction of *yin* and *yang* and the elements.

These practices are designed to build upon the exercises outlined in Parts Two and Three. All of the principles of those exercises apply as well to the nature practices. The key thing to remember is that when you are outside, you want to be as comfortable as possible in order to enhance relaxation and to enter a deeper state of meditation. Choose a comfortable, flat place (especially for standing meditation), and make sure that you are neither too cold nor too hot.

Find a place that suits you, one that seems to be "your spot." If for some reason you are not completely comfortable, it will impede relaxation and the attainment of higher levels of consciousness.

If suitable conditions are not available, all these practices can be performed inside your home (though not as effectively), so long as you can see and hear the natural world with which you are connecting.

The Practice of the Sun

Most of the world's cultures have viewed the sun as the source of all life. Taoists, too, believe that the sun is one of the most powerful and sacred forms of natural energy with which the practitioner can work. *Caution: Never stare directly at the sun*, as this will cause irreparable damage to your eyes.

Sunrise is the best time to practice this exercise. However, it can also be done at high noon and sunset, although the eyes must be kept closed throughout to avoid retinal damage.

Spring, the time of growth, is the best season in which to practice the exercise. You may do it at other periods of seasonal change as well, for almost any change means that there is an increase in the available natural energy that you can utilize.

Do not do this practice if your body feels cold because of the outside temperature. Practice in an environment that is neither too cold nor too hot, thus maintaining the balance of *yin* and *yang* within your body.

1. The best time to begin the practice is shortly before sunrise. Stand facing east, the direction in which the sun rises, and select a standing meditation posture that you find comfortable.

2. Relax the body and mind as much as you can, breathing slowly and rhythmically through the nose, with the mouth closed. Be sure you have selected level ground.

3. Stare directly at the glow before the sun comes over the horizon. Close your eyes as soon as the sun appears. *Do not at any time look at the sun!*

4. Merge the rays of the sun with your own energy. Visualize light filling your body, and feel the warmth from head to toe. Let your body feel like a sunbeam.

5. Continue to relax with an empty mind filled with sunlight. Doing this until the sun has fully risen gives you the benefit of the energy of the entire change from darkness to light.

6. Stand only as long as you are comfortable, then gradually transform the body of light that you now possess back into the material form in which you originally began the practice.

The Practice of the Moon

Many cultures recognize the moon as a powerful force. In China, the full moon symbolizes the attainment of enlightenment, the regaining of the primordial unity of the Tao. Some of China's greatest sages are said to have cured serious ailments by practicing under the mysterious light of the full moon.

The best time for the practice of the moon is in the fall when the moon is full, for then it radiates particularly powerful *yin* energy. This practice is particularly good for women.

1. You can practice under the light of the moon at any time, as long as it is not too cold outside. Select an area where the ground is level.

2. Select a standing meditation posture that is comfortable, and begin gazing steadily at the moon. Relax as much as you can, and breathe slowly, naturally, and rhythmically through the nose, with teeth together and lips slightly parted.

3. You may choose to close your eyes in order to develop your mental abilities. In your mind's eye, visualize the moon as clear and bright as it was when your eyes were open. When you can consistently hold a clear image of the moon in your mind, you will know that you are progressing.

4. Like the sun, the moon should not be thought of as a separate object far away in the sky. See it as a living, glowing aspect of your own consciousness. Absorb the glowing light of the moon into your own being, until it merges with your own inner light and you feel as if you are a moonbeam. (If there are any constellations that you are particularly attracted to, you may use them to perform the same meditation.)

5. Stand for as long as you are comfortable. Gradually extend the duration of your contemplation.

6. When you feel tired or restless, gradually return your conscious mind to your body.

7. During stressful periods, visualize the moon and remember how you felt when you were bathed in the serenity of its glowing light.

The Practice of the Mountains and Stones

Since ancient times in China, mountains and boulders have symbolized stability, strength, power, and relative permanence. The Taoist recluses of the past discovered that the optimum elevation for the development of the *ch'i* was between 800 and 1,200 meters above the surrounding territory. They thought that if you were too high in the mountains, the shortage of oxygen would require the body to struggle too hard to build the *ch'i*. At lower elevations there were more distractions and impurities in the air. In general, the cleaner and more natural the environment, the better.

1. Select a mountain near your home where you feel particularly comfortable and happy. This generally indicates that an area's natural energies are compatible with your own.

2. If there are no mountains near your residence, you may go to a park and practice beside a large rock.

3. As you walk up the mountain, try to be aware of your surroundings as much as possible. Do not focus your eyes on any specific point. Walk slowly and wait for some portion of the landscape to suddenly pull your attention toward it. Look at this area directly and see if it feels right to you. If it does, and there is a level area, or you can stamp one out with your feet, this is the place to practice on this particular day. If not, continue walking, breathing slowly and regularly, until a spot selects you. You may want to return to practice in this spot repeatedly or find another the next time you return.

4. After you are content with the feeling and beauty of your surroundings, select a comfortable standing posture. Relax and feel your feet growing into the mountain. If you are practicing next to a rock, visualize and feel the energy of the rock surrounding you while your energy surrounds the rock.

5. Do not regard the mountain or rock as a lifeless entity separate from you. Realize that it is alive, responsive, and filled with joyful energy, which it can and will share with you if you are able to relax completely. Close your eyes and feel its power surge upward through the bottom of your feet to the top of your head.

6. Continue standing as long as you are comfortable. Feel that your own body has actually become a part of the mountain. When you feel tired, gradually return to your physical form.

Feel free to improvise with different types of natural terrain. Mineral and fossil deposits are particularly good areas to practice this meditation. Avoid the extremes of hot and cold, and be as comfortable and natural as possible, or you won't feel the energy.

Calligraphy: form of the mind

The Practice of the Trees

Trees are a treasured source of energy for practicing I Chuan. The solidity of a tree, its roots connecting it with the energy of the earth, is a quality that is emulated by the practitioner. One has only to look at the roots of a tree growing near rocks or a sidewalk to realize that a tree has the tremendous power necessary to buckle concrete and separate stones. As long as our arboreal friends are not injured, they seem able to live for an indefinite period of time. For the Chinese, trees live in close harmony with the Tao.

1. You can practice with a tree in your backyard or any natural area. The energies of trees are most available at dawn or dusk, but they can practice with you at any time. In general, select a comfortable standing meditation posture as close to the trunk of the tree as possible.

2. If you are in a wooded area, walk slowly and visually scan the area without focusing on any single object. Wait for one tree to select you by suddenly becoming the attractive focus of your attention in a way that differs from all the surrounding trees. You will know when you have found your tree because you will feel more inclined to practice with this tree than with any other you have seen.

3. Once you approach your tree, notice from which direction the sunlight is falling on its trunk. If you feel tense and have recently been under a lot of stress, you may want to stand in the tree's shadow, which heightens the convergence of *yin* energy. If you feel weak or have recently been ill, you should stand in the sunlight. In any case, you should always try to stand on the most level area at the base of the trunk.

4. Whether you stand facing the tree trunk or away from it depends on the size of the tree and your personal preference. If it is a small tree, you may be able to partially encircle the trunk with your arms without actually touching it. A larger tree may ask you to stand with your back as close to it as possible without making physical contact.

5. Relax by feeling yourself breathing with the tree. Feel every part of your body gently expand and contract as you inhale and exhale naturally, smoothly, and softly. Experience the feeling that there is no difference between you and the tree. Maintain this feeling as long as you can.

6. If you get tired but wish to continue your meditation, sit down with your back

against the tree and close your eyes. Imagine that the pressure of the trunk against your back is your own spine and that tremendous energy is being transmitted into your body. Continue as long as you are comfortable. The same exercise may be done lying down with your head against the base of the tree, using leaves for padding if the bark is too rough for the scalp and neck.

7. When you have completely returned to your own body, place both hands against the trunk of the tree and slowly inhale and exhale 21 times, or a bit longer. Mentally transmit your own energy to the tree through your palms while exhaling, and take in energy while inhaling. You will know that you are doing this correctly when you feel a slight pulsating sensation directly in the center of your palms.

You may later return to this particular tree or choose another. Feel free to improvise and experiment, because you may find a particular way of practicing with trees that allows you to integrate more completely with them. Let your own body and the tree be your guide, for there is no set routine to follow. You are attempting to draw energy by integrating yourself with nature; therefore, do what seems most natural to you.

The Practice of the Wind and Rain

The wind and rain are potentially dangerous for the I Chuan practitioner. If used incorrectly, they are powerful enough to cause an imbalance in the energy of the body, which can allow you to catch cold. It is thus often best to practice indoors with an open window and to use the sound of the wind and rain to enhance your practice. If it is too cold outside—anything other than a soft summer breeze or a warm summer drizzle—you are better off doing these practices indoors.

A perfect way of practicing with the wind and rain outdoors is in a wooded area in the summer. You may combine this exercise with the practice of the trees and further enhance the results. Remember to avoid lightning storms, the most concentrated form of natural energy that is regularly visible.

1. Close your eyes and concentrate on the sound of the wind or the rain. Listen for the patterns that are created while these energies interact with the leaves, the ground, and other surfaces.

2. Choose a comfortable meditation posture and relax. Feel that your body is as light as the wind or as soft as the rain. Let the sound pass unimpeded through your mind and body. Feel the wind and rain gently caress your face. Seek to reach a point in which there is no difference between you, the sound, and the wind and rain themselves. You will know that you are doing this correctly when you feel your body expand slightly when the intensity of the sound increases.

3. Return to your body slowly and collect your energy in your lower abdomen before leaving your meditation posture. If your energy has been scattered by the sound, it must be fully balanced before you finish the practice.

The Practice of the Water

Water is an essential life force. Not only does water constitute over 80 percent of the human body, but most of the planet is covered by vast oceans, seas, rivers, and lakes. Water is an excellent source for assisting with the production of *ch'i* because its interaction with the various elements of nature (sun, wind, moon, etc.) enhances its own inherent *ch'i*. Water acts as a magnifier that is useful in focusing energy sources. By practicing near water, you can draw on its strength and use it for your own benefit.

1. Select a body of water. The ocean is perhaps the best, though the wind at the beach can sometimes be too strong. A river, a lake, or even a small brook is also fine.

2. Close your eyes and concentrate on the sound of the flowing water. Listen for the patterns that are created.

3. Choose a comfortable meditation posture and begin to relax. Feel that your body is as fluid as the water. Let the sounds pass completely through your mind and body. Flow with the water and draw on its power. Feel the water in the air around you. Seek to reach a point where there is no difference between you, the sound, and the water itself. You will know that you are doing this correctly when you feel that the water of your own body is part of the water around you.

4. If the weather is warm, you may do this practice standing in the water. This will greatly enhance your ability to draw upon its energy. In addition, standing in a moving body of water will help you develop a stronger, more rooted stance that will improve all your standing meditations. When standing in water, be sure you are in a safe place, that the weather is good (with no chance of lightning), and that you are standing in shallow water, so that the tide or current cannot take you away. You may combine this exercise with other nature practices if they apply.

5. Return to your body slowly, and collect your energy in your lower abdomen before leaving your meditation posture.

The Practice of the Rainbow

The rainbow is a symbol of divine love in cultures around the world. It represents the energy forces of higher consciousness, which may intervene positively in the fate of humankind. Rainbows effortlessly project their brilliant hues into our hearts and minds, and we cannot help but have our spirits lifted when we see one. Because of this capacity to elevate consciousness when properly used, rainbows occupy a special place in I Chuan.

1. Rainbows are uncommon, and to catch sight of one, you must be observant directly after a rainfall, when the sun's rays come peeking through the cloud cover.

2. Immediately fix your eyes on the most brightly colored portion of the arc that you can see. Hold your gaze and begin drawing the colors into your body through your eyes and the top of your head.

3. Relax into your favorite meditation posture and keep merging your mind and body with colors and light, breathing slowly and deeply, with your eyes gently focused on the brightest part of the rainbow.

4. Allow your body to become a part of the rainbow. If you like a particular color or combination of colors, allow yourself to become the hue in the same way that a chameleon takes on the shade of its surroundings. All humans are inherently creatures of light. Actively become rainbow light, and illuminate your surroundings.

5. If you can practice from the time when the rainbow is just appearing until it can no longer be perceived, without being disturbed by random thoughts, you will have greatly enhanced your level of awareness. Where was the rainbow before you saw it? Where did it go after you could no longer perceive it? You have just seen emptiness become colored form and colored form then become emptiness. This is your own true nature.

6. Do not return to your physical body. Continue to see yourself as condensed frequencies of rainbow light. Extend this feeling of joy into your daily activities.

7. When you feel doubt, remember the rainbow. Remember, you *are* the rainbow.

PART FIVE
Exercises for Common Problem Areas

Calligraphy: I Chuan

I Chuan is a practical form of physical, mental, and spiritual advancement. As you have seen, exercises are uncomplicated and easy to practice. Other than the dictum to do what is natural, it has few fixed rules or regulations.

In keeping with this practicality, I Chuan can alleviate many common problems that afflict people on a daily basis. The exercises in this section are designed to address specific physical problems when they occur.

These exercises are not designed to replace your other I Chuan practices, but to supplement them.

Heart

107

108

109

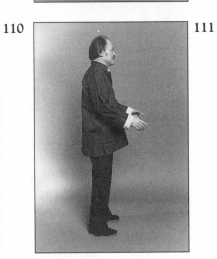

110

111

112

113

114

115

116

117

118

1. Stay calm and relaxed throughout the exercise.
2. Stand straight, feet shoulder width apart, toes pointing outward at a 45-degree angle.
3. Look straight ahead, chin parallel to the ground, throughout the practice (even when your eyes are closed).
4. Keep the shoulders and elbows down throughout the whole practice.
5. *Rocking Hands.* Keep the hands loose, palms facing inward, parallel to one another. Raise your hands to chest height and then swing them down loosely until the elbows straighten and the fingers are pointing to the ground. Maintain a moderate speed (not too fast!). Relax the whole body, paying special attention to the face and lower abdomen. (Figs. 107–113) Repeat 20 times.

119

120

6. Hold your palms face-down a couple of inches in front of your body, just above your navel. Keep the palms open but not tense. Slowly make a horizontal circle with the hands, moving them away from the body and forward until they come together, extended, in front of the body. Then, maintaining the same flow and speed, draw the hands backward until they reach their original position. (Figs. 114–120) Repeat the process. Be sure to keep the hands at the same level at all times, maintaining a slow, continuous speed. Initially do this exercise 30 times, and gradually work your way up to 50.

7. Repeat the exercise, except this time circle from inside to outside.

8. Do the sitting meditation on pages 72–73.

Knees

1. Stay calm and relaxed throughout the exercise.
2. Stand straight, feet shoulder width apart, toes pointing outward at a 45-degree angle.
3. Look straight ahead, chin parallel to the ground, throughout the practice (even when your eyes are closed).

127

128

129

4. Keep shoulders and elbows down throughout the practice.

5. *Rocking hands* 20 times (see page 95, step 5).

6. Bend your knees and extend your arms so the hands are at shoulder height. Keep the elbows slightly bent and the hands in loose fists. Slowly begin making small circles, right to left, with your hands. At the same time, match that motion with a small right-to-left circular movement of the knees. (Figs. 121–126) Do this 10 times, then repeat in the opposite direction.

7. Do the same exercise, but extend the right leg forward a distance equal to shoulder width. Then make the small right-to-left circles with the knees and hands. (Figs. 127–134) Do this 10 times, then repeat in the opposite direction.

8. Do the same exercise with the left leg forward.

130

131

132

133

134

Back

 135

 136

 137

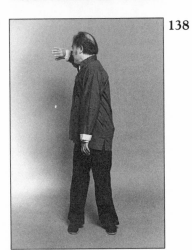 138

 139

 140

 141

 142

143

144

145

146

1. Stay calm and relaxed throughout the exercise.
2. Stand straight, feet shoulder width apart, toes pointing outward at a 45-degree angle.
3. Look straight ahead, chin parallel to the ground, throughout the practice (even when your eyes are closed).
4. Keep shoulders and elbows down throughout the practice.
5. *Rocking hands* 20 times (page 95, step 5).
6. *Back Exercise 1.* Let your hands hang loosely at your sides. Slowly raise your right arm, elbow first, and extend the arm back until the elbow is behind the head. Then extend the forearm in a scooping motion, allowing it to drop down until the fingers are pointing downward and the arm has regained its original position. Maintaining a smooth, continuous flow, repeat the process with the left arm. Keep the hands open and loose throughout the exercise. (Figs. 135–146)

 147
 148
 149

 150

7. *Back Exercise 2.* Let your arms hang loosely at
    your sides. Slowly turn your hands so the palms
    face down; then raise the arms directly in front
    of you with the elbows slightly bent. When the
    hands are a couple of inches below the
    shoulders, slowly draw the hands back until they
    are even with the front of the body. Then lightly
    push down and back until the elbows are
    extended (keep the palms facing down). Slowly
    drop the hands and bring them forward,
    beginning the same motion again in a smooth,
    flowing motion. Repeat 20 times. (Figs. 147–
    151)

 151

Stomach

 152

 153

 154

155

 156

1. Stay calm and relaxed throughout the exercise.
2. Stand straight, feet shoulder width apart, toes pointing outward at a 45-degree angle.
3. Look straight ahead, chin parallel to the ground, throughout the practice (even when your eyes are closed).
4. Keep the shoulders and elbows down throughout the practice.
5. *Rocking hands* 20 times (see page 95, step 5).
6. Loosely clasp your hands and bring them about 3 inches in front of the center of the body at navel height. Keeping the hands clasped, slowly begin

 157

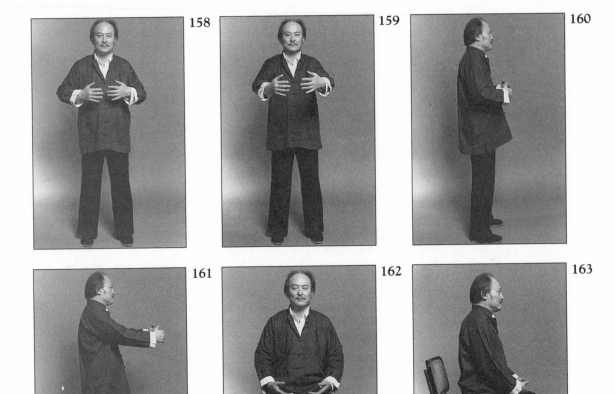

circling to your right and up. When the hands reach chest height, begin circling to the left, the hands moving across the body and then downward until they reach the starting point. Maintain a smooth, flowing movement, and don't let hands move too far to either side. (Figs. 152–157) Repeat 20 times.

7. Repeat the same exercise in the opposite direction.

8. Loosely clasp your hands and bring them about 3 inches in front of the center of the body at navel height. Slowly extend the arms forward; be sure to keep the elbows bent. Then draw the hands back to the original position. Maintain a smooth, flowing motion and be sure to keep the shoulders, arms, and hands loose. (Figs. 158–161) Repeat 20 times.

9. Do the sitting meditation (pages 72–73). However, this time keep the hands palms up, resting on the thighs a few inches away from your torso. Imagine warm water flowing over your body. (Figs. 162–163)

Sexual Energy

164

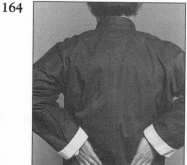

165

166

167

1. Stay calm and relaxed throughout the exercise.
2. Stand straight, feet shoulder width apart, toes pointing outward at a 45-degree angle.
3. Look straight ahead, chin parallel to the ground, throughout the practice (even when your eyes are closed).
4. Keep the shoulders and elbows down throughout the practice.
5. *Rocking hands* 100 times (see page 95, step 5).
6. Reach behind you and place your palms on your lower back, directly over the kidneys. Slowly rub the kidneys in small up-down motions 10 times.

168

169

170

171

172

Then, maintaining contact with the body, bring the palms around to the front of the body, so that the hands form a circle whose center is three inches below the navel in the center of the body. Then shake the lower abdomen lightly for 3 seconds. (Figs. 164–167) Repeat 10 times.

7. Stand with the arms hanging loosely at your sides. Slowly raise your hands, palms facing the ground, and make loose fists. Raise your hands until the forearms are parallel to the ground and perpendicular to the body. At the same time, bend the knees (no more than a few inches). The hands and knees should reach their final positions simultaneously. Then slowly drop your arms and return your knees to their original position. (Figs. 168–172) Repeat 20 times.

173

174

175

8. Let your arms hang loosely by your sides. Open your hands fully. Then, simultaneously, make a loose fist and contract the muscles in your groin area. (Figs. 173–175) Repeat 20 times.

Headache

176

177

178

179

1. Stay calm and relaxed throughout the exercise.

2. Stand straight, feet shoulder width apart, toes pointing outward at a 45-degree angle.

3. Face straight ahead, chin parallel to the ground, throughout the practice with your eyes closed.

4. Keep the shoulders and elbows down throughout the practice.

5. Rub your hands together until they get hot. Then rub your head in a circular motion, starting in the front and coming over and around the back of the head, until the hands return to the original position. Be sure to keep your eyes closed. (Figs. 176–180) Repeat 20 times.

180

181

6. Place the tip of your index finger directly in the center of the top of your head. Slowly rub this point for 20 seconds (or more or less, as you prefer). Keep the eyes closed. (Fig. 181)

Sinuses

182

1. Place the middle fingers of both hands in the indentation next to the bottom of each nostril.
2. Apply mild pressure for 20 seconds (or more or less, as you prefer). Keep your eyes closed. (Fig. 182)

About the Author

Master Yuan Pei Dong is a martial arts expert and a professional painter and calligrapher. He has studied I Chuan and other martial arts for over twenty years. He acquired the powerful methods of the late Grand Master Wang Xiang Zhai through the teaching of Wang's best disciples, Master Zhang Chang Xing and Master Yu Peng Xi.

A native of Shanghai, Master Dong was a professor of Chinese language and literature for seventeen years before emigrating to the United States in 1980. He now lives and teaches in New York City. Master Dong is one of the few people in the Western hemisphere teaching the rare inner art of I Chuan.

Princeton U-Store, NJ
Wed 29 Mar 2000
$4.88 + .29 tax
sale book with discount